AuthorHouse™
1663 Liberty Drive
Bloomington, IN 47403
www.authorhouse.com
Phone: 1 (800) 839-8640

Published by AuthorHouse 2/2/2016

ISBN: 978-1-5049-7115-7 (sc)
978-1-5049-7116-4 (e)

Library of Congress Control Number: 2016900182

Print information available on the last page.

authorHOUSE®

NO PLACE TO CALL HOME

My Life as a Palestinian Refugee

By

THURAYA AHMAD HASAN GHANNAM

An oral history transcribed by her son, Thaer Shafiq Ali Abdallah
Edited by Dorothy Buck, Ph.D.

DEDICATION

I am dedicating this book to those who have contributed to its editing and funding, to my son, Thaer Shafiq Ali Abdallah, and to the soul and memory of my precious deceased husband, Shafiq Ali Abdallah, may Allah bless him. To the rest of my children and grandchildren, may Allah protect and save them.

-Thuraya Ahmad Hasan Ghannam

FOREWORD

It has been a privilege for me to be the editor of the English language version of this story. It is a story of pain, perseverance and resilience in the face of great obstacles and loss. It is the story of a life filled with courage, faith, hope and love, laughter and joy, and above all, a story of the miraculous triumph of the human spirit. May Thuraya's story, told in her own words, be an inspiration for all who work and pray and hope for reconciliation in place of violence, hatred and retaliation and for peace with justice in Israel and Palestine and throughout the Middle East and the world.

-Dorothy C. Buck, April 2015.

ACKNOWLEDGEMENTS

I am grateful and give thanks for all those who have contributed financially, and who have given moral support to the writing of this book. It is a woman's narration of the story of a nation. I am particularly grateful and thankful to Thair Tuffaha for his support of this story, to Mr. Basheer Mahmoud Ghannam and Mr. Eyaad Assamiee for their translation from the Arabic into English, and to Dorothy C. Buck for her English corrections and revisions. I also would like to thank my brother and friend, Mr. Adnan Bin Ali, for his support and advice in the editing of this book. I am also grateful to all those who have helped me, or had a hand in ensuring the publication of this project. I also thank those who have welcomed me to America, in particular the Irish International Immigrant Center and their welcome-to-America party. With gratitude and appreciation I would also like to acknowledge:

Dr. Sheila Abdallah

Mr. Paul Provencher

Mary Ellen Provencher

Ronnie Millar (the Irish International Immigrant Center)

Abby Colbert

Jeannie Kain

Jacob Leidolf

Beth Pyles

Donna Perry

Ellen J Koretz

Faten Al Hakeem

Branwen Cook

Robert Cable

Lorraine Grzyb

Laurie Alpert

Adam Shapiro

Cathy Breen

Anne Loyer

Sarah Darghouth

Rabbi Barbara Penzner

Deborah McGill

Emad Qasrawi

Rana Awwad

Mohammed Alghool

Vivienne Shalom

Beverly Shalom

Phyllis Bluhm

Nabi Alhakim

Dr. Ramzi Nasir

Lee Traub and the late Marvin Traub

Katherine Auspitz and the Office of Michael Capuano, U.S. House of Representatives

Eklas Makkiya

Thanks to all for believing in the importance of this work.

-Thuraya Ahmad Hasan Ghannam

INTRODUCTION

Dear Readers:

This story of my life is told for my children, grandchildren and for every person of good will, that they may know the catastrophe of Palestine throughout the years. It is told in simple words, since I never went to school, although I wished to. I hope that my words are still pleasing to you.

In this book you will learn about a kind of arrogance and tyranny that exists in the world, but also about resilience and even joy. You will understand it through the story of a Palestinian woman. The Zionist Occupation deprived me of my childhood and of my innocence, and left me homeless. I lived through the tragedies and calamities as others did without a homeland and in constant migration from 1948 up to the present day. And as the days pass by, nothing good happens for Palestinians as they face daily tragedy in their struggle to live in the West Bank and Gaza under Occupation. They are still in need of ordinary life standards in every area of life. I watch what is happening to Palestine in general, and to Gaza in particular, the massacres and murders of families, and wonder at the silence of the Arab world and the global community.

May this story motivate and urge my people to remember their land and their former glory.
I pray to Allah to protect you and guide your wandering.

,,,,,,,,,,,,,,,,,,,,,
Thuraya Ahmad Hasan Ghannam
1 January 2015

CHAPTER ONE

The first journey of my life … and the Diaspora of my country

This is the story of my life. I narrate it to you honestly and with tears of tragedy. I am writing my story, and through these lines am sending it to all beating hearts longing for freedom and dignity. I am sending it to all who are zealous for their land.

I am sending it to the conscience of every Arab and Muslim, and to every human being in this world who feels the suffering of our people in Palestine. I hope that this story will move the feelings of all Muslims and everyone in the world. I am convinced that such a story will be beneficial to our country and our people. I ask Allah to protect us, our families, all Muslims and everyone in the world.

I am the daughter of wounded Palestine. I am Hajah Thuraya Ahmad Hasan Ghannam of Palestinian nationality, born in 1936 (later recorded born in 1930 by the Red Cross, due to lack of paperwork). I was born in Tira Haifa to a family consisting of my father, my mother and sisters. My mother Aisha was married to one of the villagers whose name was Qasim, and she had two daughters, Alia and Mariam.

After the death of my uncle Qasim, my mother married my father, Ahmad and she had four more daughters, my sisters Rhea, Fatima and Amenah and me, named Thuraya. We were a simple and poor family and lived in a modest house. When I was ten years old I used to walk around the neighborhood with my family in Palestine. I remember each day as clearly as if I were seeing it today.

Why wouldn't I remember it? It was my country where I grew up and lived my childhood. I used to live in Tira, Haifa and walk around the neighborhood with my family until the Zionist militias received support from the British and bombed our areas with everything they had of hardware and military power. They attacked us violently by land, sea and air. Their attacks targeted ordinary citizens and innocent civilians who did not have any weapons to defend themselves. They had only their faith in God. Moreover, I remember the days when the village of Tira fell to the Zionists, with the support of the British. The fall of Haifa city as a whole, as well as the fall of Akka were not until April 1948, which led to the fall of our village, Tira nearby.

This resulted in the displacement of many families to the nearby villages that had not yet fallen to the Zionist enemy, like Ain Ghazal and Ajzim. I was displaced with my small family and sought safety in the village of Ain Ghazal where we rented a small house where we stayed for a time until we built a small room and lived in it with my whole family for nearly two months. We used to sit and spend time with my uncles in their homes, because they owned houses of their own. After some time, relatives from Tira came to visit us and told us the story of the suffering that they faced in Haifa during the displacement. They came on foot to see us and reassure us. Their trip to us took three days. In fact we were surprised by their arrival in the village of Ain Ghazal. Of course, my father, my mother and my sisters welcomed them and washed away their fatigue with water in our small house, which we had built of mud with our own hands.

In Ain Ghazal, another story

After a short time, as we were dreaming of our return to our houses in Tira, we were shocked by the Zionist aircrafts bombing our houses in Ain Ghazal. We fled to the mountains to hide from the brutal shelling and hid under the olive trees. Once gathered there, we asked my father about my sister, Rayah, when we remembered that she had gone out to buy sugar. When my sister came back, her face was black from the bombing, and her eyes were hurt. Since then, and to this day, she suffers from severe damage to her eyes, which has led to the loss of her eyesight.

The days of the falling of the villages of Jaba, Ijzim and Ain Ghazal

I remember when the villages of Haifa fell: Jaba, Ijzim and Ain Ghazal. Before the falling of these villages, the Palestinians had requested Arab support and assistance and asked them for weapons and equipment to defend themselves. Some of the Arabs responded but they sent defective weapons that exploded in the Palestinian faces. Since most of the Arab countries were under the control of British and French colonialism, of course, these weapons and the equipment were from these countries.

I recall an unforgettable incident that happened before my eyes. Three military Israeli aircraft arrived from the east of Ain Ghazal, headed to the sea, and returned to the west of the village. The Palestinians thought that these aircrafts were from their fellow Arabs, who were coming to help and save them from this difficult situation. So they went out into the streets. The women, children, and the elderly were happy, greeting these aircraft with joy and cheering, with songs and chants, but they were shocked when these planes bombed those villages and the people destroying their houses. I saw this with my own eyes; the killing, the cutting off of heads and legs. The Zionists did this to get rid of us, which led to the fleeing of families to the caves and mountains and to the safety of the olive trees. The fact is that we did not have any weapons to defend ourselves. Sometimes we had only one gun for every ten people to use collectively.

The way to Jenin

After the Zionists' bombing, we fled from our house and our villages to a large farm owned by Nayef Al-Madhi, who had raised a white flag in front of his farm in order for the Zionists to see it. This made his farm a protected place and safe from the bombing. The people, who were terrified and afraid from the bombing and the aggression, fled to the farm. The displaced Palestinians were only women, children, and the elderly. The young men left for the city of Jenin on foot, however not of all of them reached there. Some of them were killed and others only arrived in Jenin after a long conflict with life and death due to acute shortages of food and drink.

Along with those harsh events I still remember a British man who had become a Muslim and called himself Muhammad. He was fighting the Zionists and the British with the Palestinians, and after all the villages around us had fallen to the Zionists, the British man who became a Muslim was the only person who stayed with the women, children and the elderly. He continued fighting until we could not stay on the farm anymore. After that, he rode away on a horse and said goodbye to the women, children and the elderly and left on his way from Ijzim farm to Jenin. Along the way he was assassinated by the Zionists. The next day, right after the British man left the farm, the Zionists and the British came to the farm and requested that the women, children and the elderly move to another town in Ijzim. I remember that my sister Alia requested time in order to eat as the food was ready for lunchtime, but the Zionists refused and forced the families to leave immediately for the farthest town in Ijzim. We remained in the town under the olive trees from morning until evening without food or water. The Zionists searched the women and the elderly, took all the money they had and went away having confiscated every precious item.

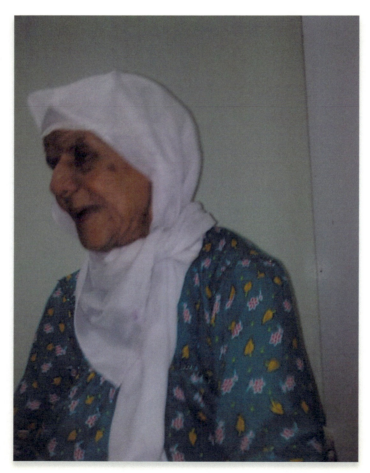

My sister Mariam who passed away in Iraq in 2012

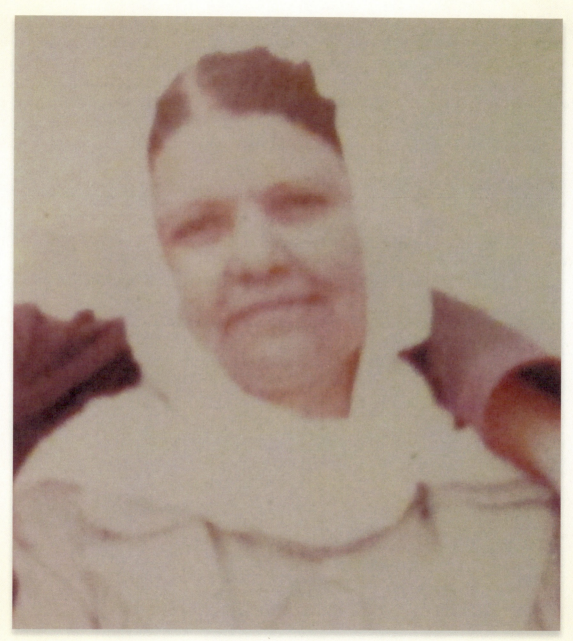

My sister Alia who passed away in Iraq in 2008

The days went by while we were left with our unknown fate and with a feeling of injustice. After that, at least five big cars came to take us. We rode in the cars from sunset until dawn and we saw destroyed cities on the road, dead bodies, and even dead animals, and the farms were burned. Then we reached the outskirts of Jenin where we sat in the open air with my parents for more than seven days without food, but the people of nearby villages supplied us with simple meals which were not enough for all of us. Then we arranged our affairs. Some lived in the buildings in the area such as schools and mosques, however my family and I lived in a village called Al-Fandaqumiya, which is located between Jenin and Nablus. We resided in that village for about three months. These events took place in 1948.

In the midst of these events and the cruelty of these days, I recall an unforgettable incident that happened before my eyes that I used to tell my children about. We had a Jewish neighbor who cried so much when we were leaving, and said to my father, "Do not go to King Abdullah, the King of Jordan, who sold you". From her words I then realized the meaning of the word treason and knew for sure that the Arab rulers had betrayed us.

I still remember that where we used to live in Palestine, before the Zionists came, there were a small number of Jews with whom we lived in peace and security. My uncles had great social relationships with them and they were visiting each other and used to meet in a tent. I will never forget these Jewish neighbors and friends. I wish that I could meet them again.

CHAPTER 2

The first migration to Iraq

For a period of time we were under attack by the Zionist enemy and we lived under very hard circumstances. Then cars came from Jordan, Iraq, Syria, Lebanon and Egypt, and asked the displaced Palestinians to register the names of those who wished to travel. Some did not record their names and stayed in Jenin, Nablus, Al-Fandaqumiya, and Balatah, while some of them agreed to travel and moved to the above mentioned neighboring countries.

It was our fate to go to Iraq because the Iraqi army asked us to go to Jenin city which was under the control of the Iraqi army that was led by General Omar Ali. We resisted the Zionists there for three months in fierce battles in cooperation with the Iraqi army. At that time the Iraqi army asked the people who were within the area of its control to leave this area. The Iraqi army accepted the young people who were able to fight. This was according to orders issued from King Faisal II, who was the king of Iraq from April 4, 1939 until July 1958. The army had promised to send the young men back to their homes immediately after the war ended.

After we had moved to Iraq in 1948, the Iraqi government at the time of King Faisal II arranged for our stay in Iraq. We were divided into three categories that were sent to different places in Iraq. The first category represented the people who were sent to the town of Basra in southern Iraq to the Al-Shuaiba Camp. The second category represented the people who were sent to the town of Mosel in northern Iraq. The third category represented the people who were sent to Baghdad, the capital of Iraq. The Iraqi government housed them in the College of Engineering at Bab Al-Moathem and in some government offices during the summer vacation. When I saw this happen, I felt that the transfer of Palestinians to distant places outside the country was a British Zionist conspiracy. I believe the Arab rulers participated in the implementation of this conspiracy.

The Iraqi government arranged our stay in Iraq. Some lived in government buildings, and some of them lived in schools. We stayed there for a limited period of time and then they took us to the army's Shuaiba camp near the city of Basra. The Iraqi army was responsible for Palestinian refugees and provided us with food. All these dramatic events took place in one year, the year of the Nakba (the catastrophe) in 1948. We lived in Basra for three years.

When we came to Iraq and got to the camp of Shuaiba, I was twelve years old. During these three years, we immigrants were engaged in our normal lives of work, study, and marriage. The Iraqi government allocated a sum of money for each individual resident of three dinars per month.

When I was fifteen years old, I got married to Shafiq in Shuaiba but because of traditions and customs I did not meet my husband before our marriage. At the beginning of my life with Shafiq he was working and he was also the goalkeeper for one of the Palestinian sports teams in Shuaiba in the region of Basra.

My marriage certificate: July 30, 1950

A year after my marriage, we moved to Baghdad where we were the responsibility of the Iraqi Ministry of Social Affairs. The Iraqi army was no longer responsible for Palestinian refugees. At that time Iraq had not signed an agreement with the United Nations Relief and Works Agency for Palestinian Refugees in the Near East (UNRWA), that was established in 1949, preferring instead to address the needs for assistance of the Palestinian refugees itself.

My life in Baghdad ... new chapters of tragedy

In Baghdad we lived in an area called Abu Sovin in the homes of the Iraqi Jews who had immigrated to Palestine!! We lived in Abu Sovin for ten years, during which time I gave birth to my children Seham, Ali, Jamal, and Khetam. Forty days after giving birth to my daughter Khetam, we moved to Al-Horyah City under the orders of the government because the former houses had become uninhabitable. We were humans inhabiting houses that were like tombs.

My husband Shafiq and I with our children Seham, Ali, and Khetam in the 1960s.

We lived in Al-Horyah City for ten years. One day, in 1962 in Al-Horyah City, my father decided to marry another woman because my father wanted to have male children. The fact that God did not grant my mother Aisha male children was God's will. So my father got married to another woman called Sidika and she gave birth to 5 daughters and three boys. Since my father was working as a guard at the ice cream factory in the region of Al-Topchi close to our house, he could support his family which had become a big family.

At this time my mother, Aisha Suleiman Ghannam, died. She was kind and had a very compassionate heart. She lived in a room in the region of Al-Topchi. Six months after the death of my mother in 1981 my father, who was born in Haifa, Palestine, also died after a long illness (1908 - 1981).

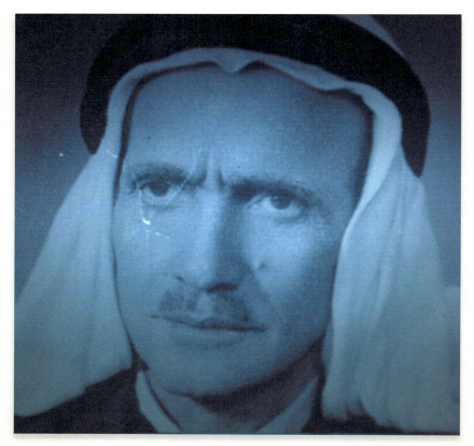

My father, Ahmad Ghannam (1908-1981). He passed away after a long illness. May Allah bless his soul.

At about the same time, I was shot and wounded in the neck by a random gunshot. The bullet is still lodged in my neck. I could not walk for two months, but I eventually made a full recovery. During our stay in Al-Horyah City, I gave birth to my children Harbyah, Khairyah, Hanan, Amer and Thamer.

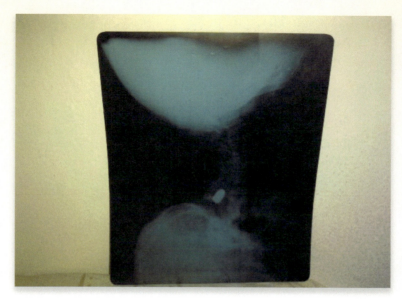

X-ray of the bullet still lodged in my neck

My children and me: Ali, Jamal, Amer, Thamer, Seham, Khetam, Harbya, and Khairya

When I was pregnant with my son Thaer, we moved to the region of Karrada to Al-Atar Street. I gave birth to my children, Thaer, Manal, Taghreed and Tariq there. We lived in a building inhabited by seven families and my family was composed of thirteen people. We lived in Karrada for about twelve years.

My children and me: Thamer, Manal, and Thaer

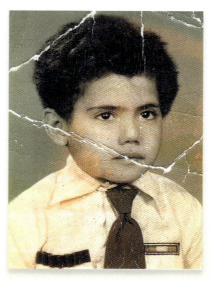

My youngest child, Tariq

During this time my husband worked for twenty-three years as a driver for the passenger transportation department and then he retired from that job. After that he worked as a truck driver in Iraq between Baghdad, Alexandria and Almahmoudiya. In addition, he worked as a political activist. He was a man with a compassionate heart. He loved animal husbandry and planting and caring for trees in the big garden of our house. In his garden there were many beautiful fruit trees like bitter orange trees, fig trees and berry trees. The large garden was full of all kinds of animals that he took care of. There were rabbits and chickens and he had a police dog named Fox.

During this time my husband's brothers and their children came to visit us and they went with my children to the garden to pick all kinds of fruits like figs, berries, and dates. They loved to climb the trees. One of the trees we had in our garden was very big. It was called a buckthorn tree with small fruit, like cherries. The children were always throwing stones at it or climbing it and the fruits were falling on the ground so that they could collect them. In spite of the fact that the tree had thorns, its fruits were delicious.

We lived a very simple and wonderful life in Karrada. Iraq is well-known for its hot weather, especially in the summer. I remember how my children used to sleep on the roof of the house because of the heat. At that time I was always cleaning the roof of the house with water. I liked the smell of the dust which was usually accompanied by cold moisture and a good odor. My husband brought a big jar with water and put it on the roof of the house and we covered this jar with a cloth bag to keep it cold during the night. This jar exists even today and is called a "zeer". We kept the zeer filled with water so that my children could drink when they felt thirsty.

The beauty of the simplicity and innocence of those old days was wonderful! Before sunset, my sons and daughters used to climb up the stairs to the roof of the house taking their mattresses and pillows to be ready to sleep in the cool weather. I made a wall of cloth between the roof of our house and our neighbor's, as we had only one roof. This was a way of showing respect for our customs and traditions. You see a beautiful and delightful sight when you sleep under the moon and the stars and the sky. During those good old days, our relatives visited us often, coming from neighboring countries like Jordan, Syria and Lebanon.

Karrada Neighborhood, Baghdad. This is a photo of an original watercolor by my son Thaer Abdallah. As you can see, Christians and Muslims lived together in harmony.

Purity of life and hearts in the Seventies and Eighties of the last century.

In the Seventies of the last century, we lived beautiful days with our Iraqi neighbors. We felt like one family with each other. We did not distinguish between Sunni and Shiite Muslims and Christians, but shared each others' joys and sadness. We always went to the Abu Nawas Park which was a park specifically for families who were eating the same kind of food, especially Al maskuf fish that is grilled on coal with hot Iraqi bread called kuras. It is so delicious and cheap.

My sister-in-law and me with our children, in the Abu Nawas Park in Baghdad, Iraq, 1960s.

Many years later, the Iraqi government moved Palestinian refugees to different neighborhoods that were separated from each other. These places did not have suitable housing. These were in the region of Alzafaranya in Al-Salam Neighborhood called Topchi. After the war of June 1967, Ahmed Habboubi, the Minister of Social Affairs and Labor, visited the shelters inhabited by Palestinians and was surprised by the misery of the Palestinians that he saw there. He sent a message to the Iraqi Council of Ministers at that time that stated, "I visited the shelters inhabited by our Palestinian brothers. I was surprised by what I saw. I am not exaggerating if I compare the houses to tombs which are inhabited by living people." They were not different from tombs. There was no place for the sun's ray's to fall. Not even a small amount of fresh air was allowed to enter the rooms from the outside in these houses. The buildings were old, cracked and dangerous for human life. Residents lived in constant anxiety and fear.

One room that had an area of 3 x 3.25 m was lived in by 7 - 12 people. The same area was used for cooking, washing clothes, washing dishes, taking baths as well as serving as the area for the children to play. There was no separate wall between one family and another and that caused boys and girls to mix. That was dangerous. Also there was the threat of communicable diseases and epidemics, especially since these places were not clean. The problem was greater than I can describe since hearing it is not like seeing it. Humans living in such places lose their humanity and life becomes impossible to continue in such places. Life in these places is like the life of animals. When I say this I feel pain and I am sure that your concern will give this issue the necessary attention to save such poor people today from the miserable situation in which they live. Despair has become part of them. They are also afraid to hope for what may save them from these harsh circumstances. They have surrendered to despair. I cannot hide my feelings of bitterness when I see the reports about children, women and the elderly whose pale faces say it all.

Thankfully, various human rights workers reported on the situation of Palestinian refugees in Iraq, and as a result, in 1968 the Iraqi State made a resolution with recommendations that Palestinians must have houses. However, this property belonged to the State, since Palestinians only had the right to live in it while they were in Iraq and had no rights to buy a piece of land for building or to request any Cooperative Estate funds.

Palestinians also weren't allowed to nominate themselves for the Council of Administration, but in 1971 they were allowed to have jobs up to the level of General Manager.

In 1980, we moved from the Karrada district to the Al-Baladiyat neighborhood, which was the name of the residential complex for Palestinian refugees in Baghdad. I lived in the Baladiyat neighborhood during the Iraq-Iran war. At that time we continually heard the sound of rockets, bombing and the warning sirens for air strikes in Baghdad. During this war, many innocent victims were killed.

During this time, my children were going to school and I used to get up early to wake them and prepare their breakfast and get their clothing ready to go to their schools. When they went to school, I would be waiting anxiously for their return, preparing their lunch. And when they returned to the house, I held them in my arms.

My husband Shafiq worked as a driver for the Japanese Mitsubishi company. He worked to support his family financially. In addition he bought a small Volkswagen taxi as another job. He drove the car between Karrada and Bab Al-Sharqi. After that he opened a small shop in Al-Baladiyat neighborhood to sell different products. He was licensed by PepsiCo, SinalCo, Crush, and 7-Up to sell soft drinks. He was a struggling, brave and socially engaged man who liked to stay up and listen first hand to the news on the radio. He loved hearing the songs of Arab singers such as Samira Said and Fayza Ahmad, and played Chess with his friends.

The Last Departure of my husband

This beautiful life and these happy days didn't continue, and even our smiles didn't last any longer. Shafiq had become ill with heart failure. We drove him daily to Ibn Al-Nafis hospital in the Iraqi zone called Al-Andalus. His heart condition gave him less and less life, and he died in 1986 after a long final illness. My husband, Shafiq, the father of my children who struggled day and night for a good life, passed away. May Allah bless him.

My husband Shafiq and I, before he passed away in 1986. May Allah bless him.

The Enormous Catastrophe.

We really prayed to Allah after the final departure of my husband, who had stood by his family as best as he possibly could. In his place, Allah gave us my eldest son, Ali, who resembled his father in striving, love and affection. Ali was the backbone of our family. In the eighties, Ali used to take us on picnics, gathering us together with our relative's families. Each family brought food to the picnic. He also used to rent a bus for us to go to a district called Salman Bak. He accompanied us to a swimming lake in a place called Al-Habania, a resort in the west of Iraq between Al-Falujah and Al-Ramadi. He married and had four children. They are Enas, Feras, Nibras and Yaser. He never left us alone. He was very kind to us. He paid visits to all of us. Ali worked for a British company called Metro-Baghdad. One night on his way to work he said goodbye to us and turning his back he drove off in his car. His car then went off the road and turned upside down near the new center in Iraq, called the Municipalities. It was the most terrible catastrophe and broke my heart. He died in 1987, a year after his father's death. He was 34 years old. His death added to the difficult burden left by the loss of my husband. Our house was crowded with grief. Our tears of lament never stopped. Ali was buried in a cemetery named Al-Ghazali. May Allah bless his soul.

Another Tragedy

Our calamities were renewed in 1991 with the war between Iraq and Kuwait. We lived under an economic siege imposed by the United States of America that continued for ten years. We suffered a lot with the loss of electricity in the hot summer and the rising prices of petroleum. We started to use generators for electricity during the duration of the war. The availability of water was also limited and there was an acute shortage of medicine. Markets closed, which caused us much difficulty in buying the necessities for daily living. We had to use black wheat mixed with sawdust because of the manipulation of the markets, high prices and cheating. I used to use our small space heater as a stove. This was called the Iraqi "sobah."

Due to the shortage of drinking water, I used to fill up the tank of water with the generating machine. I also used to get up early in the morning to do that while plenty of families were waiting to get their water in turn. We were greatly harmed by such an economic siege, but we thanked God.

The door of our apartment in Baladiyat. You can see the water tank, which I used to fill.

Another Tragedy, just as important as the previous ones.

The anguish and tragedies for us were repeated as sadness came once again. In the year 2000, my son, Jamal, left this life. He was married and had five children. His children are Rami, Fadi, Tamarah, Muhammad, and Hiba. He was a good man with a tender heart. He worked as a taxi driver. Then he worked for a cigarette company. He was attacked by the disease of cancer and passed away. He really suffered a lot with his cancer. We kept him company daily in the hospital for six months. During this time, he couldn't close his eyes because of his difficulty breathing. We shared his suffering with him too. My other sons, Amer, Thamer, and Tariq stood by him day and night in turns. They took him to the hospital every day till his last breath, on a Friday morning in 2000. May Allah bless him. In all, I lost three persons close to my heart, my husband and the father of my children and my two sons, just as I had previously lost my motherland, Palestine and my hometown, Haifa. As the years passed, all of my sons and daughters got married. They have had their own children and families. With Allah's help, I now have about 70 children, grandchildren, and great-grandchildren.

My son Ali, who passed away in Baghdad, Iraq, 1987. May Allah bless his soul.

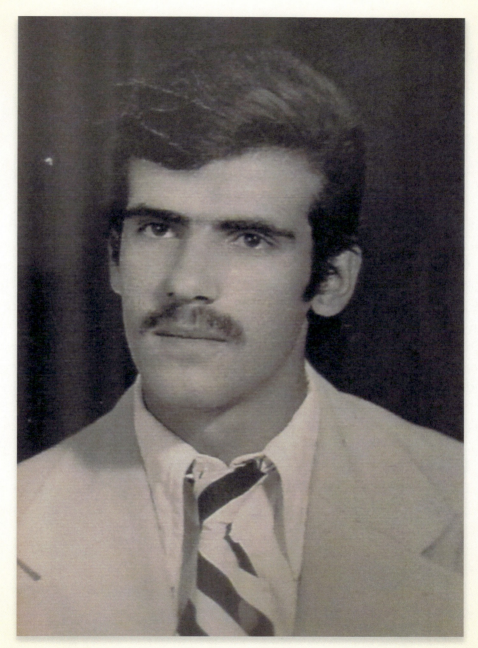

My son Jamal, who passed away in Baghdad, Iraq, 2000. May Allah bless his soul.

CHAPTER 3

The War of 2003

Through the scenes of bombing and gunfire in the eyes of my grandchildren, Allah bestowed a long life on me in order to narrate the phases of the difficulties of life that had already been determined for Palestinians as their destiny. War had been launched once again to destroy everything. I lived through the war of America and Iraq in 2003, which was much more difficult for us than the last ones. This time we gathered in one apartment. There were about thirty of us in my family. We hid in the bedrooms and in the kitchen, afraid of the saturation bombing by the American fighter planes. In our area there was no water and the electricity was cut off. At night the bombardment was intense. We used candles, surrendering totally to God, Allah, with prayers, praises and invocations. My granddaughter, Noor, ten years old, said the prayers while all the others repeated them and said "Amen" with her. In actuality, our supplication to Allah was to be able to relieve so much agony from the bombardment. Our district was attacked and battered many times. The firing of rockets reached the housing complex where we were. Many Palestinians were victims. The housing complex was bombed during the time of Saddam Hussein's rule, and the overturning of his State.

After the downfall of Saddam's State, we were subject to racial persecution. The American military forces attacked our housing with tanks and armored cars. Their fighter planes flew at low levels over the complex, especially at night. They used their police dogs as well. Fear was visible in the faces of the women and children. In fact, and historically speaking, I would say we lived through a harder and more powerful war than ever. It was the war that had sectarian dimensions provoked by the Iraqi media that led to our being targeted aggressively by Shi'i sectarian gangs.

Palestinians were assassinated, kidnapped and expelled from their homes. The media presented us as terrorists to the Iraqi people, who knew nothing about our life. They thought that we were being given special treatment by President Saddam Hussein. They were told that we were given apartments and financial aid, but in fact, we were not allowed to own anything in our own names. Palestinians had no rights. All Palestinian citizens were prohibited from owning a car, or a house, or a piece of land, or a cell phone in his/her name, or a right to vote in any election, or to join the Iraqi army or to have an Iraqi identity.

After 2003, the youth and small children were prevented from going to school. People couldn't go to work in fear for their lives because about 300 Palestinians were assassinated. Many of my relatives lost their lives, and my grandson, Rami Jamal, was abducted in 2006 by the Iraqi forces from his father's house in Al-Karadah. He was in his twenties. We haven't found him yet. We Palestinians have lost many experts and qualified people such as teachers, students, doctors and engineers, as well as children and many ordinary men and women. Some were kidnapped and their kidnappers requested much ransom from their families. The surviving Palestinians stayed in their houses because they felt unsafe given the abductions, murders, and barbaric crimes all around them. The bodies of the dead were mutilated having been tortured by different atrocious methods including drills, acid, electricity and perforations. We felt very sorry that we could not lend a hand to the wounded or drive them to the hospital. Since they were "just Palestinians" they might be killed on their arrival at a clinic. We couldn't even obtain death certificates for them. Those people who requested death documents, received nothing. Also it was hard to bury the bodies of our dead. This really happened to one of my relatives. Crimes were registered but we didn't have the media or means to make charges to the authorities so that the facts could be shown to them. Nor did we have the means to rescue ourselves from the miserable conditions in which we lived. This is because they dealt with us as if we were terrorists and belonged to the Sunni minority.

My cousin Waleed, killed by the Iraqi Militia, September 27, 2003

My cousin Jamal Saeed, killed by the Iraqi Militia, 2005.

The Legal Position of the Palestinians Post the Downfall of Iraq.

Palestinian citizens had to visit the Passport and Immigration Authority for the reinstatement of their residence in the municipalities. However, we faced difficult restrictions that were imposed on us when we sought these documents. Residence was limited to one month, with payments up to about ten thousand Iraqi dinars. We faced long waits up to midnight, maltreatment, bad words, and routine difficult bureaucratic procedures. We were subjected to all of these in order to simply be able to get a monthly residence ID. Even our children who were born in Iraq had no citizenship – they had Palestinian travel documents issued by the ex-Iraqi State. Children and the elderly were obligated to wait long hours, standing on their feet, and under the hot sun for more than five hours at a time.

Palestinian Travel Document issued by the Iraqi government

After the Palestinian families were kicked out of their houses by the Iraqi owners of the houses, a camp was established in an athletic club named Haifa Club, near to Al-Baladiyat housing complex in the municipalities. The club received many of our families.

CHAPTER 4

The Second Migration: From Iraq to Syria

Living in Iraq became very difficult for us. We then realized that we were being subjected to a planned and managed eradication by this lack of stability and security. So our life changed into a hell. There were no ordinary living standards available such as electricity, water, or sewer systems. Diseases spread all over the city. We really did live with the absence of these ordinary standards of human life. Finally, there was no other choice except to depart from Iraq for another country. We were full of sorrow that no other Arab country would accept us, except of course, for the desert and the tents.

The second migration of the rest of my family started when the Iraqi Palestinians tried to reach the first Asylum for Refugees -- Ruwaished Asylum. This camp on the border with Jordan had been established in 2003. This camp was established after a struggle with the Jordanian Government when they refused to let us be in their land, stating a political pretext. At the time, the Government used its military forces to stop Palestinians from entering Jordan. This camp was supervised by the UK, and continued for four years. Some other countries received Palestinians, like Canada, Brazil and Chile. I lived in Al-Ruwaished Camp for about two months. I left it due to the worst circumstances, desert life in my old age.

So I decided to go back to Baghdad, Iraq.

Migration To Syria and Embracing Life in New Camps

Difficulties faced us, barriers stopped us, life got crowded with our families, when killing and random abductions increased. All those events pushed my son, Thaer Abdallah, with a group of Palestinian families, to leave Iraq forever in 2005 for Syria, accompanied by an international Christian human rights organization called 'CPT', Christian Peacemaker Teams. I did not accompany him, deciding to continue daily life in

Baghdad. After a long and arduous effort, they reached the borders of Syria, where the first camp was set up. It was called Al-Tanf Camp. At first, the Syrian government refused to accept them because they had Palestinian travel documents issued in Iraq. They stayed on the borders of Syria about forty days pending the Syrian government's decision. Although they had nothing but the cold, they spent most of their days rejoicing in a way that we had all lost for many years. They really met the challenges head on. In addition, during that time, my son, Thaer fell in love with an American woman named Sheila, who was a member of the CPT. They fell in love in the desert. After many trials, including years of separation and my son Thaer's imprisonment for his human rights work, he finally got a visa and they were married in the USA. They now live there with their son, Yusef, who was born in 2011.

Al Tanf camp 2005. My son Thaer led the group and was in charge of setting up the camp with the help of the UNHCR.

Al Tanf Camp 2005. Sheila, my son's future wife, with the Palestinian refugee children. The children and their families are all now resettled in Canada.

I continued living in Baghdad until 2006, but as a result of the lack of security, and the crowded conditions in the housing projects, I and other Palestinians made the decision to find a safe destination by leaving Iraq forever, into neighboring countries. We got illegal passports, and planned our escape. Some of us left for Syria, and I was one of them. Some departed to Jordan. Some others left for Europe illegally by sea.

I arrived in Syria in 2006 with an illegal Iraqi passport. My daughter Hanan was residing in Syria and took care of me while I lived there. During my time in Syria, I had three surgeries: eye surgery, surgery to remove kidney stones, and gallbladder surgery. I was happy to have my daughter by my side. Also, while in Syria I remember human rights activist Cathy Breen from New York came to visit me. Cathy Breen advocates for Iraqi and Palestinian refugees and spoke to UNHCR on my behalf.

Peace activist Cathy Breen, with me and my son Amer in Syria in 2006

I lived in Syria for five years. During this time all my sons left me to live in other countries. They are Amer, Thamer, Thaer, and Tariq. I stayed in Syria with a broken heart every time I thought of them. My eyes were full of tears for their departure. In 2009 I made my decision to go to Al-Tanaf Camp, which was between Syria and Iraq. This camp was looked after by the United Nations High Commission for Refugees. It was my hope to be together with my children or to see their faces again, and to regain my great happiness with them. I lived in the camp nearly a year.

Circumstances of life in the camp were very difficult owing to inadequate health care and the hot dusty atmosphere that my old age couldn't tolerate. I was cared for there by my daughter's sons, Muhammad and Tawfeeq. In the camp many things happened. There were fires, since our tents were so flammable, windstorms and heavy rain storms that caused the tents to be flooded more than once. The torrents penetrated the tents and drowned our necessities. I cleaned it all up myself. Moreover there was a prevalence of deadly insects such as snakes, and scorpions in summer, and chilling cold in winter.

When I was in the camp, my daughters wanted to come and visit. I had six daughters living in Syria, Jordan, Norway, Yemen and Iraq. In order to visit me, they all met in Damascus where they got a car to be able to come to me. For us, this is a kind of obedience to one's parents. I had been so keen to hug them, and to spend time with them. Unfortunately, the Syrian authorities wouldn't allow them to enter the camp. They needed security approval from Damascus.

I waited with patience at the border to see my daughters. Sadly, they turned back to get the required security approval. I invoked God not to prevent me from seeing my daughters before I die. I prayed, "God, I didn't see my daughters for so long." I waited for months, day and night, for hours, in order to meet them. I spent most of the time on a rock waiting to catch sight of them. Occasionally I prepared tea and food and cleaned everywhere in the tent as every day passed by.

Al Tanf Camp 2009. This is a painting of me, waiting at the border to see
my daughters. My son Thaer painted this in oil colors.

This lasted for three months. Finally, three of my daughters received the approval. I lived in Al-Tanf Camp about one year.

Al Tanf camp, 2009.

In 2010, we were given the approval by the Syrian Authorities to enter Al-Hol Camp. Al-Hol Camp is located in the north of Syria. It was established in 2005. I lived in this camp for three years in difficult conditions, especially in the summer when the sun is very hot and there are a lot of insects and snakes. It became harder and harder and I couldn't even breathe well due to the dust from the windy sand storms. One day, a sand storm surged up and smothered me, but they were able to drive me to the clinic. This was in the summer, but in the winter we got chilled because our houses were built of cement and clay which didn't resist either the cold or the heat. However, we became accustomed to these impositions and our difficult situation so we didn't feel the agony.

Al Hol Refugee Camp 2010

To live through this bitter situation and to forget the pain, I made a small farm around my house in the camp. I planted trees and especially grapevines, "Dawaly", on the roof. I also planted different vegetables like parsley, celery, onions, tomatoes, etc. I tried to plant some flowers too. I raised some small yellow chicks. It was a pastime during these serious conditions of life while waiting for a new life in the diaspora.

Al Hol Refugee Camp – Raising Chickens

Al Hol Refugee Camp 2010 – My vegetable garden

Life in Al-Hol Camp......Settled in for a Long Wait.

In spite of the simple life in Al-Hol Camp, we persisted in recreating life according to our national traditions and customs. During this time my daughter Seham was able to come and visit me.

A house of prayer was built for praying and fasting. In Ramadan, we exchanged visits, particularly with the old ladies. Life rose up to a higher level of tranquility and the feeling of being settled. So much so that I and my grandson were able to walk through the camp and its outskirts full of great joy. Sometimes I sat on a high hill reflecting on my memories of Palestine and Iraq. I sang songs and recited verses of poetry for afflicted Palestine and its children, the boys and girls that I constantly longed for. In 2011, Syria had a new era of grievances. I had nothing to say except that we belong to Allah, the Best Ever Protector.

Al Hol Refugee Camp in Syria. Reflecting on memories of Palestine and Iraq.

Al Hol Refugee Camp, 2011.

Sunset at Al Hol Refugee Camp

CHAPTER 5

Migration to Turkey

After we had settled and finally found some peace in the Syrian camps -- peace that we had missed for so many years -- the situation began to be worse due to the outbreak of the uprising against Bashar Al-Assad's government in 2011. We all knew that revolution would be violent, and sure enough events escalated quickly. As Palestinians, we feared the armed fighting between the Syrian protesters and the Syrian state. Al-Hol Camp was bombarded by the state's fighter planes under the pretext that the camp was hiding rebel fighters. By then, our life in the camp had become unsafe. There was no one to take care of us or help us except God.

In February of 2013, my grandson Muhammad and I, along with other Palestinian families in the camp, decided to escape into Turkey. We were 14 persons, men and women. I won't ever forget that we had a pregnant woman with us. We arranged with a smuggler to take us into Turkey. At midnight, I walked by foot for six hours straight with my grandson and his friend, Ahmed Khalefa. He was a brave young man. They were in their twenties. They had to help me a lot to walk because of my old age -- I was in my seventies. I walked through heavy mud in the dark. The smuggler asked me to go back. He thought I was too old to walk. In reaction, I turned him down saying, "I won't go back. We have walked half way. So I will go forward, not back." To climb a mountain I used my grandson as a support. Sometimes he carried me on his back. In coming down the mountain we crossed through a deep pool of water. He crossed the pool while I was on his back. His brave young friend carried our luggage along with us. We crossed the pool with difficulty. It was so dark. We came to barbed-wire fences that we had to go over. I tried, but the wire caught my clothing, tearing them. Having gone through such pain with an unknown destiny in the terrible darkness, we somehow arrived at a safe place. We spent the rest of the night in a cottage made of clay.

Early in the morning, we had our smuggler go to the city center to hire a car. While we were standing on the road, a Turkish Police car passed. They arrested us and took us with them. We weren't allowed to enter the police station in our shoes because they were full of water-saturated clay. Then they put us behind bars in detention because we entered their country illegally. Here I must tell the truth, that during the questioning they treated us in a good way. I have to note that the Turkish officer played with one of our children. He did it affectionately. This shows that they knew about humanity. Then they sent us to a camp in Adana, a Turkish city. Syrian immigrant families were living in the camp, so they gave us permission to leave that camp and go to another Turkish city called Mersin where we rented an apartment. We were able to get our necessities, and our souls were safe.

On the way to Adana, safe in Turkey at last.

We arrived in Turkey in February 2013.

My grandson Muhammad and I. He risked so much to help me across the border.

My boys came to see me. Thaer, my son, whom I hadn't seen for 7 years, came from the USA. About a month later, Tariq, my youngest son, came from Norway. I hadn't seen him for 3 years. I made sure that they were healthy. And they made sure of my health too. Then they left me to return to the countries where they work. They offered for me to travel with them, but legal procedures are difficult for Palestinians. Now I was living with my grandsons, Muhammad and Tawfiq, Tawfiq's wife, Hiba, and his lovely newborn boy, Mustafa. I spent my time in the apartment. I did some work by hand such as knitting some clothing. I knitted clothes for my grandson, Thaer's son, Yusef, whom I hadn't seen yet except in photos on Facebook. As I am so old, I hoped to meet them once again. I lived with the hope that I would one day meet all of my children, their wives and my grandchildren, and be able to live with them under one roof. It is still also my hope to live in peace and safety, that wars will end and migrations will stop. Everything is in the hands of God, Allah. Nothing is impossible for Him.

My great-grandson Mustafa – my grandson Tawfiq's son. Mersin, Turkey, 2013.

Greeting my son Tariq, whom I had not seen for 3 years, and my son Thaer, whom I had not seen for 7 years.

My son Thaer and I when he visited me in Turkey, 2013

I spent a lot of time in the apartment knitting clothes for my grandchildren,
including Yusef, Thaer's son whom I had not yet met.

03/06/2013 02:12

I also spent time helping my daughter-in-law Hiba by buying produce
in the marketplace and helping with the cooking.

My grandson Mustafa was growing up. Here we are in Mersin in 2014.

CHAPTER 6

The Last Journey

I lived in Turkey for more than one year. It was a peaceful time, but we were still in-between, with no permanent security or sense of home. After I lived in Turkey, with the help of my son Thaer and his wife Sheila and the Irish International Immigrant Center, I was able to get an immigrant visa and ticket to the USA. One of the documents I was required to submit was a police clearance certificate from Israel. Since Palestine was under British mandate at the time that I resided in Haifa, Palestine, it was impossible to get this document. Israel did not exist at that time. Thanks to the volunteer lawyers at the Irish International Immigrant Center, we were able to overcome this and many other obstacles. My son came to Turkey in June 2014 to accompany me to the interview at the American Embassy in Ankara, Turkey. It was a 14-hour ride from Mersin to Ankara by train. While Thaer was here, and before my interview with the American Embassy, Thaer went to the Embassy of Palestine in Ankara, Turkey and explained the situation of the police clearance certificate requirement. The Embassy of Palestine issued a document in lieu of the police clearance certificate from Israel. We arrived at our appointment with the US Embassy at 7:30am and waited several hours until the counselor finally saw us at 4:00pm. The entire interview was five minutes. The counselor who interviewed me was very pleasant and told me I was very close to being approved for my visa. One month later, I was issued a visa to the USA.

My visa to the United States

Suitcases packed and ready to leave Turkey for the United States, to live with my son Thaer and his family. July 2014.

My son Thaer and I standing outside the airplane, preparing to leave Turkey for a new life.

I did not turn back. I put myself in the hands of God.

My son, Thaer, accompanied me from the Adana Airport in Istanbul, Turkey, to Boston in the USA. The trip was really hard for me because it took us ten hours. I arrived in Boston in America on July 29, 2014 and I met my grandson, Yusef. May Allah bless him. It was Yusef whom I promised to meet and dreamed to meet. This has been achieved with God's help and that has made me so glad. In the airport we were welcomed by Sheila's father, Mr. Paul Provencher. We picked up Sheila from work on the way home. Paul's wife, Mary Ellen, received me with open arms and flowers once we arrived home. My grandson Yusef also welcomed me at the door.

Yusef and Mary Ellen welcoming me to my new home

My daughter-in-law Sheila, my grandson Yusef, and Sheila's parents MaryEllen and Paul, on my arrival to the USA

My grandson Yusef opens the gift that I brought for him.

Yusef showed me my new bedroom. July 29, 2015

People of different faiths welcomed us, too. Phyllis Bluhm and Vivienne Shalom, Jewish-American friends of my son Thaer welcomed me with flowers. I was also welcomed by some Iraqi families and have gotten to know them. Thanks to all of them.

Vivienne Shalom and Phyllis Bluhm – Jewish-American artists and
friends of my son Thaer – welcomed me with flowers.

The Irish International Immigrant Center had a celebration for immigrants and I was so happy to be there. I really owe them a vote of thanks for their humane work. I thank every employee in the organization, especially the lawyers, Abby Colbert and Jeannie Kain, the executive director of the organization, Mr. Ronnie Millar, and the also the employees in the office of Massachusetts State Representative Michael Capuano, especially Kate Auspitz, for their help in obtaining my documents.

My son Thaer and I with Jeannie Kain, Evelyn Brito, Janey Tallarida and
Ronnie Millar at the Irish International Immigrant Center (IIIC).

The executive director of the IIIC, Ronnie Millar, is holding a small Irish flag
that I knitted for them in gratitude for their work on my case.

Now I'm living with my son, his wife Sheila, and their child, Yusef. I have been taking time to relax, pray, cook, and knit. My son Thaer also has taken me around to different places in Boston. During my first winter here, they had more snow than they had seen for many years!

Since I've been here, I also now have a new primary care doctor, Dr. Anu Mehra. I like her very much as she is very patient and caring towards me.

Yusef and I playing in the yard
of his grandparents' home.

Yusef, Sheila and I relaxing, August 2015.

Teaching Yusef how to knit.

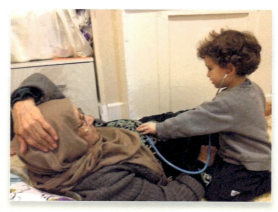

Yusef likes to pretend to be a doctor to take care of me. One day he told Thaer,
"When I grow up I want to stay home and take care of Tayta" (that's me).

I had never seen the snow. Boston had more snow than they had seen for many years.

Thaer and Yusef and I at Sheila's parents' home.

My doctor, Anu Mehra. She is very kind and caring.

I still have my hope to go back to my motherland, Palestine, and to my village, Haifa, the cradle of my life. I hope to meet my children and grandchildren in my lovely home in Palestine. In conclusion, I say in truth that this has been my journey in life. I have narrated all of it for you in order that you know the extent of the agony we suffered. I ask Allah, the One, the only One, to bring peace to our lands and among all people, to make an end to war and to fear, and to bring us all together again.

This is an expression of thanks and respect for everyone who stood by me, for everyone I love, my relatives and kin. ***May Allah help us to do good.***
~THURAYA AHMAD HASAN GHANNAM

Yusef and I at home.

AFTERWORD

There is an aspect to Thuraya's life story that she did not speak about in detail in this story. A whole separate story was the journey of her son Thaer and his wife Sheila, a peace activist and now physician, that began in Baghdad after the US invasion of Iraq in 2003. As Thuraya said, "they fell in love in the desert." From there, they too experienced a painful, frightening, dangerous and ultimately miraculous and inspiring journey from a desert tent to a refugee camp and to a new life in the United States. For the next several years they undertook an extraordinary effort to free Thaer's mother, Thuraya, from the cycle of migration from one country and refugee camp to another and bring her safely to the United States.

Thuraya's enduring wish was to one day see all of her children and their families together again, in one place. This did not come to pass. At the time of this printing, two of her children are still living in daily peril – in Baghdad and Damascus, respectively. Her other children are scattered in Norway, Sweden, Algeria, New Zealand, the United States, and Jordan.

Thuraya did not include the toll that her life journey took on her physical health, nor the lack of medical attention that is an inevitable reality for refugees forced to flee in the face of overwhelming war and danger. Thuraya arrived in the US in 2014 and was finally able to receive good medical attention and to experience the joy of living in the safety and warmth of family, with her son and daughter-in-law and her grandchild. On April 16, 2015, nearly one year after arriving in the United States, Thuraya suffered a sudden devastating stroke, and returned home to Allah. May her soul rest at last in the peace and love of Paradise.

-Dorothy Buck and Sheila Abdallah

THE WANDERER

"You,
who are traveling to foreign lands,
your own homeland is better.
Oh my beloved,
I am afraid you will leave,
obtain possessions, live with others . . .
and forget about me."

-Thuraya Ahmad Hasan Ghannam

Printed in the United States
By Bookmasters